I want to be a Chef

Other titles in this series:

I WANT TO BE A
Chef

DAN LIEBMAN

FIREFLY BOOKS

A FIREFLY BOOK

Published by Firefly Books Ltd. 2012

First Printing

Publisher Cataloging-in-Publication Data (U.S.)
(Library of Congress Standards)

Liebman, Daniel.
    I want to be a chef / Dan Liebman.
[24] p. : col. photos. ; cm.   I want to be.
ISBN: 978-1-77085-003-3
ISBN: 978-1-77085-004-0 (pbk.)
1. Cooks -- Juvenile literature. 2. Cooking -- Vocational guidance – Juvenile literature. I. Title. II. Series.

641.5023 dc22   TX652.5L543 2012

National Library of Canada Cataloguing in
Publication Data

Liebman, Daniel
    I want to be a chef / Dan Liebman.
(I want to be)
ISBN 978-1-77085-003-3 (bound)
ISBN 978-1-77085-004-0 (pbk.)

1. Cooks--Juvenile literature.
2. Cooking--Vocational guidance--Juvenile literature.
I. Title. II. Series: I want to be

TX652.5.L54 2012   j641.5023   C2011-905887-1

Published in the United States by
Firefly Books (U.S.) Inc.
P.O. Box 1338, Ellicott Station
Buffalo, New York, USA, 14205

Published in Canada by
Firefly Books Ltd.
66 Leek Crescent
Richmond Hill, Ontario, L4B 1H1

Photo Credits:

Front Cover: © Erwin Purnomo Sidi/Dreamtime

© George A. Walker: pages 6, 7, 8, 9, 12, 14-15, 16, 20, 23, back cover

Mike Miller: page 21

Istockphoto © Giorgio Fochesata: 10-11

© Erik Isakson/Tetra Images/Corbus: page 13

© Monkey Business Images/Deamstime: pages 17, 22

© Imagegami/Dreamstime: page 18

© Newmedia/Dreamstime: page 19

The publisher gratefully acknowledges the financial support for our publishing program by the Government of Canada through the Canada Book Fund as administered by the Department of Canadian Heritage.

Printed in China

What do chefs do? They prepare food for people to enjoy.

The word "chef" means "chief." A chef is in charge of a kitchen.

Chefs plan menus. A menu is a list of foods that are served in a restaurant.

Finding fresh food is an important part of the chef's job.

A chef's day is a busy one. Some chefs start work early in the morning. They often work on weekends and holidays.

People train to become chefs. They learn their job by going to school and working in restaurants.

A chef needs to have a good sense of taste. This salad needs a little more salt and pepper.

At home, people cook for a family. In a restaurant, a chef prepares meals for many people.

There are different kinds of chefs. Pastry chefs make cakes, pies, breads and fancy desserts.

Chefs use different tools. They use sharp knives to cut food.

The sous (pronounced "soo") chef is the chef's assistant. The sous chef works under the main chef. "Sous" is the French word for "under."

This pizza chef creates hundreds of pizzas a day. He'll make your pizza just the way you like it.

Chefs make sure that the food is tasty. The food must also look nice on the plate.

Some chefs write cookbooks. Chef Ernie has just written a book about fresh food.

Chefs need to take care of their pots, pans, knives and other equipment.

This young chef is making her favorite recipe. You can make it, too. See the next page.

Yummy Chocolate Chip Cookies

Makes at least 50 cookies!

What you need:

One adult to help, plus:
two mixing bowls and an electric mixer
measuring cups, measuring spoon, teaspoon
ungreased cookie sheet

2¼ cups all-purpose flour
1 teaspoon baking soda
½ teaspoon salt
1 cup butter or margarine (softened)
¾ cup white sugar
¾ cup light-brown sugar (packed firmly)
1 teaspoon vanilla
2 eggs
2 cups chocolate chips (semi-sweet)

What you do:

1. Preheat the oven to 375°.

2. In the first bowl, mix together flour, baking soda and salt.

3. In the second bowl, blend the butter, the white sugar and the light-brown sugar. Then add the vanilla. Then add the eggs, one at a time. Continue to mix until everything is light and fluffy.

4. Blend in the flour mixture. Make sure everything is mixed well – there shouldn't be any lumps.

5. Stir in the chocolate chips.

6. Use a "rounded" teaspoon and drop the cookies onto the baking sheet.

7. Bake for 8–12 minutes. The cookies should be golden.

8. Cool the cookies on the cookie sheet for a couple of minutes.

9. Pour a glass of milk and enjoy your chocolate chip cookies.